THE ULTIMATE SEX MANIACS JOKE BOOK

by
Larry Wilde

BANTAM BOOKS

NEW YORK · TORONTO · LONDON · SYDNEY · AUCKLAND

THE ULTIMATE SEX MANIACS JOKE BOOK

A Bantam Book / May 1989

Illustrations by Ron Wing.

ISBN 0-553-28013-9

Published simultaneously in the United States and Canada

Bantam Books are published by Bantam Books, a division of Bantam Doubleday Dell Publishing Group, Inc. Its trademark, consisting of the words "Bantam Books" and the portrayal of a rooster, is Registered in U.S. Patent and Trademark Office and in other countries. Marca Registrada. Bantam Books, 666 Fifth Avenue, New York, New York 10103.

PRINTED IN THE UNITED STATES OF AMERICA

O   0 9 8 7 6 5 4 3 2 1

For John Ziccardi
The ultimate Italian sex maniac

Contents

Lewd Libidos

What would you call a low-class motel?
A humpty dump!

*   *   *

Do most men prefer panty hose or bare legs?
Something in between!

*   *   *

What would you call a girl who drops her pants every time a man drops a hint?
A suggestion box!

*   *   *

What do you call a man with syphilis, herpes, AIDS, and gonorrhea?

An incurable romantic.

*   *   *

Wayne went into the hospital for a routine circumcision. When he woke up from the anesthesia a large group of doctors were gathered around him.

"What happened?" asked Wayne.

"Well," said Dr. Palmer, "we made a small mistake. There was a slight mix-up and we performed the wrong operation on you. Instead of a circumcision we gave you a sex-change operation. We cut off your penis and gave you a vagina."

"That's terrible!" sobbed Wayne. "You mean, I'll never again experience an erection?"

"You will," said the doctor, "but it'll be somebody else's."

*   *   *

What do a meteorologist in a snowstorm and a woman's sex life have in common?

They're both concerned with how many inches and how long it will last.

*   *   *

METALLURGIST

A man who can take one look at a platinum blonde and tell whether she is virgin metal or common ore.

* * *

Why can love be so intoxicating?
It's often made in the still of the night!

* * *

What's the difference between a light bulb and a sports car?
It's easy to screw in a light bulb!

* * *

What would you rather be, a light bulb or a bowling ball?
Depends on whether you'd rather be screwed or fingered.

* * *

What's the difference between a pregnant woman and a light bulb?
You can unscrew the light bulb!

* * *

How many mice does it take to screw in a light bulb?
Two.

How many sex therapists does it take to change a light bulb?

Two: One to screw it in and one to tell him he's screwing it in the wrong way.

* * *

How many fleas does it take to screw in a light bulb?

Two. But first you have to get them into the light bulb!

* * *

What would you call a sex party where everybody falls asleep?

A snorgy!

* * *

When is premature ejaculation a serious problem?

When it occurs between "hello" and "what's your sign?"

* * *

What's the best way to get excited?

Think hard!

* * *

"Just one more kiss, darling."

"On an empty stomach?"

"Of course not, right where the last one was."

*   *   *

Did you hear about the coffee bean that said, "I'd like to be made instant?"

The other said, "Not me, I prefer the regular grind."

*   *   *

Why do jokes about oral sex choke people up?

Because they're in bad taste!

*   *   *

How does a horny, ugly man describe his sex life?

Fist or famine!

*   *   *

PYLON
What a nymphomaniac might say
at a nude beach party.

*   *   *

A large midwest meat and poultry packing firm held its annual convention in San Francisco. Eddie, one of the employees, had quite a hot romance with Marcia, a pretty hotel waitress, during the week. When it was time for him to go home, Eddie promised the girl he'd come back to her as soon as he could get away.

Two months later, when Marcia hadn't heard from Eddie, she decided to go to him. When she got to the huge packing plant, she went to the personnel manager and said, "Will you please tell Eddie Johnson that I'm here."

"We have three men here by that name," said the manager. "To save me some trouble, will you describe him?"

"Oh, he's short, kind of heavy, and has a thick mustache."

"And does he dress in loud clothes?"

"Yes, he does."

"Eddie Johnson, the pheasant plucker."

"That's him," nodded the girl. "And he's a wonderful dancer too."

* * *

Why are cowgirls bowlegged?

Because cowboys like to eat with their hats on.

* * *

What's the scariest thing for a nudist?
Frying bacon!

* * *

The candidate for mayor was making a speech denouncing the proliferation of X-rated video cassettes. He stood before the crowd and said, "I rented one of these cassettes and was shocked to find by my count five acts of oral sex, three of sodomy, a transsexual making love with a dog, and a woman accommodating five men at once. If elected, I vow that tapes such as these will no longer befoul our fair community." Then he asked, "Are there any questions?"

Eight people shouted up, "Where'd you rent the tape?"

* * *

Why is it estimated that only 99% of all people masturbate?

The other 1% were either taking the poll or answering the door!

* * *

Jennifer was terribly lonely and on Christmas Eve eagerly waited for Santa to show up. When he finally scrambled out of the chimney into her living room, she asked, "Santa, will you please stay with me?"

"Ho, ho, ho, gotta go," said Santa. "Got my presents to deliver."

Jennifer removed her robe and repeated her request.

"Ho, ho, ho," said Santa, "gotta go, gotta go."

The woman slipped out of her panties and bra and whispered, "Santa, won't you please stay with me?"

Santa replied, "Ho, ho, ho, gotta stay—can't get up the chimney with my dick this way!"

What tool is about six inches long, has hair on one end, gets stuck in a fleshy crack, and rubbed back and forth before white juicy stuff comes out?

A toothbrush!

*　　*　　*

When a man takes off his pants in a hotel room, what's the first thing to hang out?

The DO NOT DISTURB sign!

*　　*　　*

What's six inches long, has two nuts, and can make a woman fat?

An Almond Joy!

*　　*　　*

Why is pubic hair curly?

If it was straight, it would poke your eyes out.

*　　*　　*

What's the best thing to come out of a dick?

The wrinkles.

*　　*　　*

ORAL-GENITAL RELATIONS
Being head over heels in love.

* * *

There once was a gal named Jill
Who used dynamite sticks for a thrill
   They found her vagina
   In South Carolina
And bits of her tits in Brazil.

* * *

Judy was an unattractive but wealthy single girl. Tired of sitting at home every night, she placed an ad in the personal column of the *New York Times:*

   Rich, sex-crazed, admittedly
not good-looking woman wants man for
   quiet liaisons.

The day after the ad appeared, she received a letter by Federal Express. Her heart pounding with excitement, she tore open the envelope. Anxiously, Judy's mother, who was visiting, asked, "So? Who's it from?"

The young woman replied, "Papa!"

* * *

A Cleveland yuppie couple hired Rosalie, a cute young Polish maid. Rosalie seemed to enjoy her work until one day, without warning, she gave notice.

"Why do you wish to leave?" asked the woman. "Is there anything wrong?"

"I just can't stand the suspense in this house a minute more," said Rosalie.

"Suspense? What do you mean?"

"It's the sign over my bed," said the Polish girl. "You know, the one that says, 'Watch Ye, for Ye Know Not when the Master Cometh.'"

* * *

How do you know when you've had a great blowjob?

You have to pull the sheets out of the crack in your ass.

* * *

Fenton ran over a cat on the freeway and cut off its tail. When the highway patrolman arrived, Fenton was trying to tape the cat's tail back on. So the officer gave the poor guy a ticket for retailing pussy on a public road.

* * *

What is the perfect job for a sex maniac?
Comparison shopper in a red-light district.

*   *   *

Doug and his fiancée Helen were sitting on a sofa. He noticed the cat playing with a tassel and said, "After we're married, that's what you'll be doing to me."

Helen looked down and then slapped Doug right in the face.

The cat was licking its tail.

*   *   *

CAT OBEDIENCE SCHOOL
A place where they teach your pussy
how to handle itself.

*   *   *

What is the sweat between Dolly Parton's tits called?
Mountain Dew.

*   *   *

Why did the snowman pull his zipper down?
He heard the snow blower was coming.

The lingerie manufacturers were getting together in Atlantic City for their annual convention. Murray talked Sharon, one of the models, into coming up to his room.

"How about fooling around a little?" he asked.

"Hold on," said the blonde. "I'm just a poor working girl. You got fifty bucks, maybe we could get together."

"All right," he agreed. "But on one condition."

"What?"

"That we turn out the lights and I can boff you as many times as I want and take all the time I want."

Two hours later she whispered into his ear, "Gee, you're making love better than ever, Murray."

"Murray, hell!" cried the guy on top of her. "I'm one of his friends. Murray is out in the hall selling tickets!"

*   *   *

What do you say to a premature ejaculator who has diarrhea?
"Easy come, easy go!"

*   *   *

What do you get when you cross a kleptomaniac with a nymphomaniac?
A fuckin' thief!!

*   *   *

Why does Dr. Pepper come in a bottle?
'Cause his wife died.

*   *   *

What to do about fallout?
Reinsert and shorten your stroke.

*   *   *

What's the difference between a 300-pound woman and a moped?
A lot of fun to ride but you wouldn't want your neighbor to see you riding one.

*   *   *

In Illinois, when an old guy romances a 15-year-old girl, it's Romeo and Joliet.

*   *   *

Have you heard about the girl who was so modest she always eats bananas sideways?

*   *   *

What do a Xmas tree and a man with a vasectomy have in common?
Both have ornamental balls.

*   *   *

There was a young fellow named Locke
Who was born with a two-headed cock
    When he'd fondle the thing
    It would rise up and sing
An antiphonal chorus by Bach.

*   *   *

DANCING
A naval engagement without
the loss of seamen.

*   *   *

Comedian Orson Bean got screams with this beaut on Johnny Carson's show:

An anthropologist in Africa was trying to teach a native tribesman English. He took him into the forest, pointed to various objects, slowly said their names, and had the native repeat them. He pointed to a tree, said, "Tree," then the native slowly repeated, "Tree."

Pointing to a gorilla, he said, "Gorilla," and the native repeated, "Gor-ill-a."

He pointed to a lion and said, "Lion." The native said, "Li-on."

Soon they came to a clearing where a couple was copulating. The embarrassed anthropologist didn't know how to describe it and said, "Man riding bicycle."

Instead of repeating the phrase, the native took his blowgun and killed the sexually involved man with a poisoned dart.

"Why did you kill him?" asked the anthropologist.

"Because him riding *my* bicycle," replied the native.

Harold owned a porno sex shop in Hollywood. When he had to go to Kansas City on personal business, he asked his friend Charlie to run the store.

"But how will I know what to charge?" Charlie asked.

"Don't worry about it," said Harold. "Just get the best price you can. I'll be back Tuesday."

That afternoon a Polish woman came in, and after looking around, said, "How much is that white eight-inch rubber dildo?"

"Eh, eh, fifty dollars," stammered Charlie.

"I'll take it," said the woman.

The next day she returned, looked around awhile, then said, "How much is that twelve-inch black dildo?"

"Eh, eh, seventy-five dollars," hemmed Charlie.

"Okay."

The next day she came back and said, "How much is that red, white, and blue one?"

"That's a hundred dollars."

"I'll take it."

Harold arrived on Tuesday and wanted to find out how his friend had handled the business.

"Not too bad," said Charlie. "I sold a white dildo for fifty dollars. The black one for seventy-five. And my thermos for a hundred.''

*   *   *

Why do truck drivers make great lovers?
They know the best places to eat!

*   *   *

What's a clitoris?
A female hood ornament.

*   *   *

What company is the leading manufacturer of vibrators?
Genital Electric.

*   *   *

What's the main difference between men and women?
Women must play hard to get; men must get hard to play!

*   *   *

What do you call a woman who makes beds in no-tell motels?
Minute Maid.

* * *

What's the difference between oooh and aaah?
About six inches.

* * *

Condom Concoctions

What's the height of precaution?
An old lady putting a condom on her candle.

*   *   *

What do you call a 200-foot rubber?
A condominium.

*   *   *

What do coffins and condoms have in common?
They both have stiffs in them, only one's coming and one's going.

*   *   *

CONDOM
A device to be worn
on every conceivable occasion.

* * *

Scott had a crush on Trudy for months. He was filled with excitement and anticipation when she invited him for dinner with her family. Scott was so optimistic, he stopped off at the drugstore beforehand to pick up some condoms.

At dinner Scott was asked to say grace, and to Trudy's surprise he prayed for nearly ten minutes. "I didn't know you were religious," she whispered to him over the mashed potatoes.

"And I didn't know your father was a pharmacist," he hissed back.

* * *

What do elephants use for condoms?
The Goodyear blimp.

* * *

Why was the rubber flying through the air?
It got pissed off.

The following incidents can only be described as a true sign of our times:

A young boy walked into a drugstore and shouted to the druggist, "Gimme three Trojans!" Then he whispered, ". . . and a pack of cigarettes!"

Two boys were walking to school.
"Guess what?" asked Tommy. "I found a condom out on the veranda."
"What's a veranda?" asked Robby.

*   *   *

What do you call wearing a condom to have anal sex?
Brown bagging it!

*   *   *

There was a young man of Cape Horn
Who wished he had never been born.
    And he wouldn't have been
    If his father had seen
That the end of his rubber was torn.

*   *   *

CONDOMINIUM
A prophylactic for midgets.

A Cherokee chief sat in front of his teepee. His youngest boy approached and said, "Father, how do we Indians get our names?"

"It's very simple, my son," replied the chief. "Your cousin was born when the sun was coming up, so she was named Rising Sun. Your brother was born by a running brook, so he was called Running Brook. Why do you ask, Broken Rubber?"

*   *   *

Cynthia was told by her mother to have intercourse with her boyfriend Glenn so he would marry her.

"But what do I say?" asked the girl.

"When you're through and he leans backward, simply say: 'What'll we name the baby?' and then he'll have to propose."

That night after intercourse, Cynthia followed her mother's advice and asked the question. Glenn finished, threw the condom out the window and said, "Well, if he can get out of that, we'll call him Houdini."

*   *   *

Pauline had been pregnant for 22 months! She went to Dr. Jessop and he was amazed that the woman hadn't given birth. Finally the day arrived and the baby was born. The M.D. decided to get to the bottom of this phenomenon and asked the baby, "Why did you wait twenty-two months to be born?"

"Because of the bad weather," said the baby.

"What bad weather?" asked Jessop. "It's been very nice these past few months."

"Well," said the baby, "everybody comin' in here had their rubbers on!"

* * *

Druggist: These rubbers are guaranteed.
Customer: But what if they break?
Druggist: Well then, er, the guarantee runs out.

* * *

Mitch and Kathi, a yuppie married couple, were planning to take a cruise for their vacation. Kathi sent Mitch to get her some Dramamine. Mitch went to the drugstore, and while he was there, picked up some condoms. On his way home Mitch made several stops and somehow lost his purchases.

The next day he went back to the drugstore. The druggist filled the order for condoms and Dramamine. As he handed the bag to Mitch he said, "Mister, I got to ask you a question. If screwing makes you that sick, why don't you just jerk off?"

* * *

What kind of birth control does Mr. Spock use?

A vulcanized rubber.

* * *

What do you do with 365 used condoms?

Melt them down, make a tire, and call it a Good Year.

*　　*　　*

While walking up a street, McGinnis was hit on the head by a used condom thrown out of a second-story window. He stormed into the house and demanded to know who was in the room above.

"My daughter," said the owner of the house.

"Is she alone?" asked McGinnis.

"No, my intended son-in-law is with her, why?"

"No reason, I just thought I'd tell you that your intended grandson had a bad fall."

*　　*　　*

Beneath a contraceptive vending machine in a Kentucky rest room someone scrawled: "Don't buy this chewing gum! It tastes like rubber."

*　　*　　*

Did you hear about the two condoms that were passing a gay bar and one said, "Wanna go in and get shit-faced?"

*   *   *

Did you hear about the 4-year-old boy who knocked up the maid?

He punctured all his father's condoms with a pin.

*   *   *

Kelley stomped into a drugstore on Monday morning and shouted at the manager, "Friday night I came in here and bought a gross of condoms. Later, I counted them and found five missing."

"Sorry to have ruined your weekend, sir," said the manager.

*   *   *

McCord came down out of the hills and paid his first visit to the big city. While he was walking down the main street he saw a woman smoking a cigarette from a holder.

"Lady, what's that thar thing?" he asked.

"It's a protector," she smirked.

The hillbilly entered a drugstore and asked the clerk, "Do you sell protectors?"

"Yes. What size would you like?"

"Oh," he said, "one to fit a camel will do!"

Bradley was being shown through a rubber manufacturing plant by the sales manager.

He paused by a complicated-looking machine that was making odd sounds.

First a *fft* and then a *ping*. "What does this machine make?" Bradley asked his guide.

"That makes nipples for baby bottles," replied the manager. "When it goes *ping*, it punches the hole in the end."

The next machine was similar but with a different sound pattern. It went *fft, fft, fft,* and then a *ping*.

"What does this machine make?" asked Bradley.

"Prophylactic rubbers," was the reply.

"Well," said Bradley, "the *fft, fft, fft* I can understand, they form the rubber. But why the *ping* on this machine?"

"Listen," replied the guide, "we can't let our nipple business go to hell!"

Thurlow entered a drugstore and asked the woman clerk for a male attendant. She assured him she wouldn't be embarrassed, so Thurlow asked for some condoms.

"What size?" asked the woman.

"I don't know. Do they come in sizes?"

"Come in the back room, here," she said, taking him to the rear of the store. "Put it in. All right, size seven. Take it out. How many do you want?"

Thurlow left the store in a daze. He met his pal Grier and told him about it. Grier immediately went to the drugstore and pretended to be embarrassed, to want condoms and not know the size.

The woman took him in the back and said, "Put it in. All right, take it out. Size eight. How many do you want?"

But Grier didn't take it out. He stayed right where he was until he reached a climax. "Well, how many do you want?" asked the woman again.

"Oh, I don't want any right now," he said, "I just came in for a fitting."

* * *

CONDOM IMPOTENCE
When a rubber turns your
dubber into blubber.

RED RIDING HOOD
A Russian condom.

*   *   *

Kirby was sterile. His wife wanted a child desperately. They agreed to vacation at a Florida hotel where the husband would find a suitable stranger to get her pregnant.

The second night of their stay in Palm Beach Kirby found Stein, a salesman, at the bar, and, pretending to be a friend, offered him a "real hot number" up in room 612.

Stein accepted. Kirby felt terrible but consoled himself with the knowledge that he'd soon be a father.

An hour later Kirby saw Stein getting off the elevator and rushed up to him.

"How was it?" he asked.

"Fantastic!" said the salesman. "But she was so easy, I couldn't get over the feeling there might be something wrong, so I used a condom."

*   *   *

Written on men's room wall:
Use contraceptives! No deposit—no return.

*   *   *

* * *

The newlyweds stopped at a farmhouse bed and breakfast for the night. By noon the next day they were still not up so the farmer yelled that it was last call for breakfast.

"Don't worry about us," called the groom, "we're living on the fruits of love."

"Okay," screamed the farmer, "but quit throwing the damned skins out the window—they're choking the ducks."

* * *

On the wedding night the bridegroom used a condom that slipped off inside the bride. He fished for it unsuccessfully with a broom straw, which also slipped in. Then he tried a toothpick to get the straw and it disappeared. Nine months later the baby was born wearing a raincoat and a straw hat, and carrying a cane.

* * *

Did you hear about the guy who went into the drugstore to buy one rubber?

He was trying to quit.

* * *

Guido walked into a drugstore that was being tended by the owner's somewhat prudish wife. "May I have six contraceptives, miss?" he asked.

"Don't 'miss' me," she replied.

"Okay," he said, "better make it seven."

*   *   *

Why did they call Ronnie Reagan the prophylactic president?

He gave us a feeling of safety while we were being screwed.

*   *   *

Psychological warfare is the best way to deal with the Soviets. Send a plane over Russia and drop millions of extra-large condoms—14 inches long and 5 inches wide. On each box print: Made in America. Size small.

*   *   *

A condom manufacturer is presently negotiating with a TV network to do a commercial with this slogan:

IF YOU WANT CHILDREN, THAT'S YOUR BUSINESS;
IF YOU DON'T, THAT'S OURS!!!

Ted was having an affair with a married woman. They were in bed going at it furiously when they heard a car pulling into the driveway. "My God!" cried the woman. "It's my husband! He'll kill you!"

When the back door opened, Ted jumped out the window stark naked. It was raining, and he hid in the bushes trying to figure out a way to get home. Suddenly he noticed a group of joggers coming up the street, and he fell in beside them.

One jogger looked at him and said, "You always run in the nude?"

"Oh, yeah," said Ted. "It really gives you freedom of movement."

The jogger took another look. "You always wear a rubber?"

"Oh, no," said Ted. "Only when it rains!"

Berkowitz, a fabric salesman, stayed overnight in a small town with a pretty girl. He had no condom, so he used a silk handkerchief.

Several years later he was passing through the same town and spotted a little boy who looked almost exactly like him. "Well," said Berkowitz, "you're a fine little fellow."

"I ought to be," said the boy, "Mama says I was strained through a silk handkerchief."

* * *

Bolton went to a drugstore for some condoms and found a woman in attendance. "What size do you want?" she asked.

"I don't know," he replied.

"All right, come behind the counter and let me see." She measured the customer with her hand and then shouted to an assistant, "Size three, Martha. No, better make it four. No, no, seven, Martha. No, no, eight! Martha, bring the mop!"

* * *

What did the Kotex say to the condom? If you break, we both go out of business.

*   *   *

Dr. Fuller gave Dumbrowski some condoms. "You use these and your wife won't have any more children," said the physician. "But don't use them dry. Wet them with a glass of water."

Four weeks later Dumbrowski returned to the doctor's office. "Hey, Doc, those things you gave me were no good," complained the Polack. "I used them like you said—not dry—in a glass of water; and now when I go to the toilet, I blow balloons and make sausages, but my wife is pregnant."

*   *   *

Donetti stopped a young fellow on a street corner and said, "Gotta match?"

The youngster searched through all his pockets, pulling out a half-dozen tins of aspirin but no matches.

"Whatsa matter, headache?" asked Donetti.

"No," said the boy. "Every drugstore I went into had women attendants."

*   *   *

Know what kind of contraceptive the fashion-conscious man is wearing these days?

Brooke Shields.

Fallwell was standing in a railroad station holding two babies in his arms. An elderly woman kept asking him the names and sexes of the two babies. To all her questions he replied politely, "I don't know, madam."

"How does it happen that you don't know your own children's names," snapped the old woman, "or whether they're a boy or a girl?"

"I'm not the father of these children," replied Fallwell. "I'm a condom salesman and these are two complaints I'm taking back to the factory."

*   *   *

A duck went into a drugstore and asked for a condom.

"Cash?" asked the clerk.

"No," said the duck, "just put it on my bill."

*   *   *

A Pawnee buck went into a huge chain drugstore and told the clerk he wanted a drum.

He was taken to the toy department and shown all kinds of drums which received a flat no. In desperation, the clerk showed him his last item.

"Here," he said, "is just what you want. A war drum."

"No wantum war drum," grunted the Indian. "Wantum piece drum . . . cundrum!"

* * *

Yellow Bird walked into a drugstore and said to the owner, "Me need'um rubber."

The druggist handed him a condom.

"Me need'um aspirin," said the Redman.

The druggist gave him an aspirin.

Yellow Bird unwrapped the rubber, dropped the tablet in the condom and swallowed both of them.

"Hey, chief," said the amazed druggist. "What're you doing?"

"Me gottum fuckin' headache!"

* * *

Sergeant Major MacCreery walked into a Glasgow drugstore and took a beat-up condom out of his kilt. "How much, mon," he asked the proprietor, "would it cost to fix this?"

"Let's see," murmured the druggist. "I could launder and disinfect it, heat weld the holes and tears and insert a new elastic in the top. It'd cost you almost the same price as a new one."

MacCreery said he would think it over.

He returned the next day. "Ye've convinced me, mon," he announced. "The regiment has decided to replace."

* * *

A Scotsman loaned his friend Jock a condom and then asked for it back. "Why, I threw it away," he said.

"Where? Do ye think we could find it again?"

"Hardly," said Jock. "I threw it out the car window on the highway."

"Eh, mon, you shouldn't ha' done it. Thot belonged to the bowling club."

* * *

Dean and Jeffrey, two American tourists in France, stopped a gendarme on a Paris street corner and complained about the behavior of the druggist down the block. ''We went there to buy some prophylactics,'' said Dean, ''but the druggist didn't speak English and we couldn't make him understand what we wanted.''

''Oui, monsieur,'' nodded the officer.

''I tried to commmunicate by example,'' said Jeffrey. ''I exposed myself to him, put some money on the counter, and pointed to my organ. He still didn't get the point, so my friend did the same.''

''Did he understand then?'' asked the gendarme.

''He smiled like he did,'' grumbled Dean. ''Then he just opened his fly, took out the largest penis I've ever seen, and scooped up the money.''

47

Femme Fetishes

Lance stopped the car on the edge of a secluded road. He turned to his date and said, "It's Valentine's Day. If I try to make love to you, will you yell for help?"

She cooed, "Only if you really need it."

* * *

"I just gotta know one thing," said Daryl. "Am I the first man to sleep with you?"

She said, "You will be, darling, if you doze off."

* * *

Peggy, a pretty airline attendant, went into a hardware store for a wall-mounted makeup mirror. The clerk wrapped it up.

"Do you want a screw for that?" he asked.

"No," she replied, "I want to pay for it, but I wouldn't mind going a couple of times for that microwave over there!"

* * *

Marla, a scrumptious New York model, married a man paralyzed from the neck down. A surprised girlfriend who knew Marla loved sex asked her how she could have made that choice.

"You don't understand," said the model. "Pedro's got an eight-inch tongue."

"An eight-inch tongue?"

"And even better, he's learned to breathe through his ears."

* * *

What's the difference between a sin and a shame?

It's a sin to stick it in and a shame to pull it out.

* * *

ASPHYXIATION
A fanny fetish.

* * *

Maxine yearned to become a career woman, and no one seemed to be able to talk her out of it.

"Listen," suggested her best friend, "men are hard to come by. You might be left out in the cold."

"Don't be silly," she said, "there's plenty of fish in the sea."

"Maybe so—but be careful your bait doesn't go stale."

* * *

Said the Brassiere: I'm the best. I cover what men admire.

Said the Panties: I'm the best. I cover what men desire.

Said the Slip: Will you two shut up— I've been up all night!

* * *

"How about it, honey? What do you say? C'mon!" he coaxed.

"Stop asking me and get started," she cried. "Or I'll get dressed and go home!"

*   *   *

Did you hear about the girl who refused to bring her date home to her apartment because she didn't have a negligee that was fit to take off?

*   *   *

"Do you believe in free love?" the psychiatrist asked the girl.

"Well," she replied, "I never gave anyone a bill."

*   *   *

Bart, a tall, good-looking Wyoming cowboy, was putting the make on a Reno showgirl.

"How about a kiss, honey? It'll be a feather in my cap."

"Stick around," said the girl. "I'll make you an Indian chief."

*   *   *

Why do women have more trouble with hemorrhoids than men?

Because God made man the perfect asshole.

*   *   *

McNally was dating Dorothy for the first time. As they cruised down a dark and lonely country road, McNally leaned over and whispered in her ear.

"No," snapped the girl.

McNally drove a little farther. Soon he leaned over and whispered in her ear again.

"No," she said.

McNally kept it up, and on the sixth try Dorothy said, "Okay, pull over to the side of the road."

"Sure will, baby," he obeyed.

Dorothy reached under her dress, took off her panties, handed them to McNally and said, "All right. Here they are! Now get into them!"

What's long and hard and excites a girl when she's finally lucky enough to get on it?

The road to success!

* * *

VAGINA

The box a penis comes in.

* * *

Fenwick, the Marketing V.P. in a computer corporation, noticed how bright and shiny his next-door neighbor kept his car.

"How do you manage it?" he asked him.

"Simple," replied the neighbor. "I use my wife's worn-out panties to polish the car."

Since Fenwick was unmarried he decided to ask his secretary for a pair of hers. The next day he called her into his office.

"Miss Jensen," he asked, "I have a personal question to ask. What do you do with your panties when you wear them out?"

"Why," she blushed, "if I can find them afterward, I put them back on again."

The morning after
　　The night before
Tammy came home
　　At the hour of four.
The innocent look
　　In her eyes had went
But the smile on her face
　　Was a smile of content.

* * *

Have you heard about the Satellite panties?
　They're for gals who think their ass is out
of this world.

* * *

What would you call a virgin on a water
bed?
　A cherry float!

* * *

Jason held the gorgeous blonde in his
arms and drooled, "I love you, dear, as no
man has ever before."
　She said, "Funny, I can't tell the difference."

* * *

Shari loved sex. Unfortunately, the poor girl was unable to find a man who could satisfy her.

"If I were you," suggested her friend, "I'd go to Italy. I've heard the guys there are the greatest lovers in the world."

Shari hopped the next plane to Rome. As soon as she arrived, she put an ad in the paper offering a thousand dollars to any man who could completely satisfy her. After auditioning a number of virile young Romans, she decided on Antonio.

They got off to a lively start, and for the next five hours they made love continuously without letup.

Then, after the twelfth time, Antonio paused long enough to catch his breath.

"Phew!" he gasped.

"Look," snapped Shari. "Did you come here to talk or to screw?"

* * *

With Clio you never
Know what's next.
Ain't she cute?
She's oversexed!

* * *

Nicole and Matthew met·in the cocktail lounge of a Palm Beach hotel and she casually asked him about his plans for the evening.

"Well," he said, "I'm going to find a nice, willing girl, invite her up to my suite, mix some drinks, turn out the lights and then make mad, passionate love to her. What do you think of that?"

"It's a great idea—if you ask me."

* * *

Bob: What would you do if I tried to put my arms around you?

Amy: I'd put up a fight.

Bob: What would happen if I tried to kiss you?

Amy: I'd put up a fight.

Bob: And what would you do if I tried to—

Amy: Listen, how long do you think a girl can keep on fighting?

* * *

What's the best thing on a woman?
A man.

Erin returned home from a date very late, complaining of an ache.

"What's the matter?" asked her mother.

"I have a pain in my shoulder," she said. "I must have wrenched it."

"Where did you and Rick go this evening?"

"We just took a ride through the old veterans' cemetery. That's where I developed this ache. Will you please take a look at my shoulder, Mom?"

Her mother ran her fingers delicately across the stiff area.

"Well?" inquired Erin. "Is it all right?"

"Your shoulder seems okay," she answered, "but your back is named Roger Quade—and it died in 1917!"

58

During a wild party at a Long Island country house, Roxanne had too much to drink and strolled outside for some air. Getting to a grassy field, she lay down to watch the stars. Roxanne was almost asleep when a cow, searching for clover, carefully stepped over her. Groggily, she raised her head and said, "One at a time, boys, one at a time."

* * *

INTELLECTUAL GIRL
One who can think up excuses that her boyfriend's wife will believe.

* * *

Russ spotted a gorgeous redhead at a country-club cocktail party. He sidled up to her and whispered, "I'd sure like to get into your pants."

"Sorry, you can't," she replied. "There's already one asshole in there."

* * *

A sex-starved passenger exposed himself to the stewardess as he boarded an airplane. She snapped at him, "Look, buster, I want to see your ticket, not your stub."

Sal was making love to his girl for the first time, in the backseat of his car. After he finished, he said, "If I knew you were a virgin, I would've taken more time."

His girlfriend said, "If I knew you had more time, I'd have taken off my panty hose!"

* * *

NUDIST CAMP
A place where nothing goes on.

* * *

Harriet was afraid of needles. Dr. Griffin had tried for ten minutes to convince her that this would not be painful. "I tell you this won't hurt," he kept saying.

"Someone once said the same thing to my sister," she snapped, "and now she can't button her coat."

* * *

The fairy godmother warned Cinderella that if she didn't get home from the dance by midnight, she'd turn into a pumpkin.

Cinderella met a real good-looking guy at the dance. He said, "Listen, I'd like to get to know you better. Why don't you come to my place for a nightcap?"

Her watch read 11:45. "I'm sorry, I have to be home by midnight," said Cindy. "By the way, what's your name?"

He replied, "Peter, Peter Pumpkin Eater."

"On second thought . . ."

The boss was surprised to hear that his secretary Maureen had joined a nudist camp. "You? A nudist?" he asked.

"Please!" she snapped. "We don't use that word. We call ourselves 'sunbathers.'"

One day Maureen came to work in great pain. She could hardly walk to her desk, and when she finally got to her chair, she sat down slowly and very carefully.

"What's wrong?" asked the boss.

"I'm going to a dance at the sunbathers' club tonight," she explained, "and I've got my hair up in curlers."

* * *

Two Las Vegas showgirls were chatting in the dressing room.

Coral: I was never so insulted in my life!
Sue: What did the louse do?
Coral: He drove me straight home!

* * *

There was a young lady named May
Who strolled in the park one day.
    She met a young man
    Who screwed her and ran,
Now she goes to the park every day.

* * *

He needn't be rich or a spender
As long as his love's true and tender.
　　He needn't be bright
　　But if he's Mr. Right
That's the night I'll surrender my gender.

*　　*　　*

"When Bernie and I get married," said newly-engaged Karen, "we're going to Trinidad to see what it's like."

"Don't be silly," said her girlfriend. "It's the same all over!"

*　　*　　*

An anxious mother was lecturing her young daughter about sexual morality.

"If you're ever tempted while out on a date," she warned, "don't forget to ask yourself this one question: Is one hour of pleasure worth an entire lifetime of shame?"

"Gee, Mom," asked the girl, "how do you make it last an hour?"

*　　*　　*

OVERHEARD AT HOLLYWOOD PARTY
She: Gosh, I'm hungry for a man.
He: (eagerly) Well, I'm a man.
She: Look, I said I'm hungry, not starved!

*   *   *

Harold struck up a conversation with an exceptionally attractive blonde in a Third Avenue singles bar.

"How about you and me stepping out tonight?" he whispered in her ear.

"Well, I don't know," she hesitated. "My mother warned me about going out with strangers."

"Aw, c'mon, we'll have a great time."

"Well . . ."

"Look, I promise not to hug you or kiss you or even put my arms around you," he assured her. "I'll be a perfect gentleman."

"Mister," she cried, "you just talked yourself out of a helluva date!"

*   *   *

Gerald had only one eye when he married Heather. She was lovely, refined, and he assumed a virgin. However, on the wedding night he learned different. For hours Gerald berated her for not telling him beforehand that she wasn't a virgin.

"You shouldn't complain about my loss," said Heather. "You've got only one eye."

"Maybe so, but my enemies did this to me."

"Well," she retorted, "my friends did this to me!"

66

TEN-INCH ERECTION
Double-digit inflation.

* * *

At Pimlico Racetrack Lucy and June were examining the horse they were about to bet ten dollars on. Suddenly they were shocked to see the stallion displaying the most prominent mark of his horsehood.

Lowering her voice, Lucy said to her friend, "Let's not bet on him—he can't win. His mind certainly isn't on business."

* * *

There was a young girl named Marie
Who romanced each man she did see.
    When it came to the test
    She wished to be best
For practice makes perfect, you see.

* * *

"Is it in?" he asked.
"Yes," she said.
"Does it hurt?"
"No."
So she bought the new pair of shoes.

* * *

Andrea had a heart like the United States Navy. It was open to all men between the ages of 18 and 35.

* * *

Written on the wall of a Washington, D.C., ladies room:
Support Women's Lib
Make him sleep in the wet patch.

* * *

Virgil, the farmer's son, married Marla, an oversexed chorus girl. Virgil was literally overpowered by the girl. He'd been in Las Vegas at a tractor-and-farm-implements convention and had fallen into her clutches. Marla, down on her luck, was looking for a bit of security. On the first night of her honeymoon she grabbed the naive Virgil and threw him down on the bed, kissing him passionately.

"Say, were you ever married before?" he asked.

"Yes, once," admitted Marla.

"What happened to your husband?" gasped Virgil.

"He died," she moaned, squeezing him tightly.

"He didn't die," stammered Virgil. "He's hiding!"

* * *

Lusty Lechers

Angelo sat in the confessional booth. The priest said, "Tell me, my son, do you lust after women?"

"No," said Angelo. "Only before."

* * *

What's the definition of *macho*?
Jogging home from your vasectomy!

* * *

"Listen, Vic," said his father, "at your time of life, there are no more excuses for this playing the field. It's time you thought about taking a wife."

"You're right, Dad—whose wife shall I take?"

* * *

LECHER
A big dame hunter.
A guy who enjoys life, liberty and
the happiness of pursuit.

* * *

Did you hear about the cautious lech who, upon discovering that his gorgeous date had forgotten to take the Pill, decided to give her a tongue-lashing?

* * *

A Dayton shoe salesman named Bert
Was attracted by every new skirt.
    Oh, it wasn't their minds
    But their rounded behinds
That excited this lovable flirt.

* * *

Kenny was just winding up his account of the previous evening's activities. "And when I kissed her good night, her whole body arched."

"Did she say you could see her again?" asked his buddy.

"I don't know. Her thighs were blocking my ears."

* * *

Theron telephoned the FBI and got a special agent on the line.

"What can I do for you, sir," asked the Fed.

"I've been getting threatening letters in the mail," said Theron. "That's against the law, isn't it?"

"It certainly is," said the government man. "Do you know who's been writing them?"

"Yeah," said the lech. "My girlfriend's husband."

* * *

What should a girl bring if her boyfriend invites her over for a bite?

Her knee pads!

A Tennessee hillbilly boy called off his wedding three days before it was supposed to take place. "What went wrong, all of a sudden?" asked his father.

"Paw," said the boy, "Ah been feelin' 'round in Ina Mae's pants, and Ah found out she's a virgin. That's why Ah decided not to marry her."

"You done right, son," said the father. "If that gal ain't good enough fer her own kinfolks, she ain't good enough fer us neither!"

* * *

Vito stepped into the booth and confessed, "I made love twelve times last night."

The priest said, "That's a serious offense. Was the lady married?"

Vito replied, "Three of them were."

* * *

PROFESSIONAL LECHER
A working stiff.

* * *

What do you call an athlete making love?
Jock in the box.

Augie picked up a beautiful girl at the bar of his Fifth Avenue hotel. After some time and many drinks later, they wound up in his room. The girl slowly disrobed while Augie ogled. She was magnificent. He went over, picked up her clothes and started to throw them out the window.

"Hey, what're you doing?" she demanded.

"Honey," he said, "if you're as good in bed as you are to look at, by the time I'm through with you, these clothes will be so out of fashion you wouldn't want to be seen in them!"

*   *   *

RELATIVE HUMIDITY
The sweat from your balls
that runs down your sister-in-law's legs.

*   *   *

"Boy, does that new steno wiggle her buns when she sashays down to the boss's office."

"If you think she shakes her caboose walking down the hall, you ought to see her with a passenger aboard!"

*   *   *

Man's greatest inventions are few
Though experts are prone to rate two
　　As vitally clever—
　　The wheel and the lever—
But lechers all say it's the screw!

*   *   *

Handsome, young Frankie showed up at his favorite watering hole swathed in bandages. "What happened to you?" asked a friend.

"I held up a train," said Frankie. "It was a bride's train, and it seems I held it up too high."

While touring a small Middle Eastern country, Sirkin, Massaro, and Greene decided to visit the sheik's palace. They passed the sheik's harem room where his 101 wives were sitting topless. The three men began enjoying themselves but were soon caught by the palace guards.

They were brought to the sheik and stripped naked, with their hands tied behind their backs. The sheik exclaimed, "You shall receive a punishment to fit the crime. You will be castrated."

He asked Sirkin, "What do you do for a living?"

"I'm a butcher," said Sirkin.

The sheik said to his huge bodyguard, "Mohammad, you will chop it off."

The sheik then asked Massaro, "What do you do?"

"I'm a fireman," he replied.

The sheik commanded, "Mohammad, you will burn it off."

The sheik turned to Greene and asked, "And what do you do for a living?"

Greene smiled. "I make lollipops!"

*   *   *

*　　*　　*

Lecherous Leo cornered his girl Bernice in the backseat of the car and was trying to make the connection. She kept resisting and pushing him away. Still he persisted. Finally Bernice became annoyed and gave him a violent shove.

"Leo," she said, "what's come over you? You've always been so restrained and so gentlemanly."

"I know," said Leo. "I just can't help it. I'm trying to give up smoking."

*　　*　　*

What's the first thing you do after a great date?

Brush your teeth with a comb!

*　　*　　*

What would you call it if you looked up a girl's skirt and got a funny feeling that you'd looked up there before?

A déjà view!

*　　*　　*

How is a lecher's view like a door?
When he's not pushing it, he's pulling it!

78

* * *

There was a young *gaucho* named Bruno
Who said, "Love is all that I *do* know.
   A tall girl is fine
   A short one's divine
But a llama is *numero uno*!"

* * *

What's the best thing to do if you're on a date with an annoying nymphomaniac?
Give her a vibrator and tell her to buzz off!

* * *

How can you tell if a lecher is a masochist?
He beats his meat with a hammer!

* * *

Did you hear about the guy who complains that this winter has been so cold it takes him 45 minutes to get his girlfriend started?

* * *

"What kind of lover is Andy?"
"You kidding? This guy's gone down on everything but the *Titanic*!"

Clovis went to a country dance and decided to have some fun with the girls. He attached a mirror to the toe of his shoe. When he danced with a gal, he asked the same question, "If Ah can guess the color of the panties you're wearin', will you give me a kiss?"

Intrigued, the gals took up the challenge.

After several kisses and a good deal of fun, one girl, Nancy Lou, decided to return the trick. She went to the ladies room, took off her panties and then waltzed out to the dance floor with Clovis. Nancy Lou dared him to guess the color of her panties.

"Well, darlin', Ah can't tell rightly about the color of yore panties," said Clovis, "but Ah can say one thing for sure: you ain't no blonde!"

* * *

REAL LECHER
A guy who can carry 2 cups of coffee
and 12 doughnuts at one time.

* * *

Lance, the Long Island lecher, got his
face slapped an awful lot. But then, he
made out better than most guys simply because of a bold and brash technique. Lance
handed every girl he met a business card
with his name, phone number, and this
message printed on it:
>All I want is one small chance
>To work my way into your fancy pants.
>Your fuse box is there, and if hot-to-trot,
>I'll cool it for you with what I got.
>So remember any time your fuse is lit,
>Give me a call and I'll do my bit!

* * *

There was a young bachelor of Ware
Who had an affair with a bear.
>He explained, "I don't mind
>For it's gentle and kind
But I wish it had slightly less hair."

* * *

Here are a few approaches used by some of the ranking lechers:

"Let's play graveyard . . . I feel like burying a stiff!"

"What'll you have? Gin and platonic . . . or would you prefer scotch and sofa?"

"Are you serious? Honey, I need you like a whore needs a pussy stretcher."

"I could squeeze ya till you break!"
So he gave her a tight hug, and sure enough, he felt her crack.

* * *

"How does Wayne make out with chicks?"
"He's such a good stud. He's trapped more beavers than Grizzly Adams."

* * *

What's the worst problem a lecher can have with sex and booze?
Every time he has sex, the girl boos!

* * *

Why didn't the "flasher" retire?
He wanted to stick it out for another year.

Gomez, a free-spending, irresponsible Bronxite, ran up a large bill in Miller's swanky men's shop, buying racks of expensive suits and assorted shirts and ties. The exasperated owner of the store kept sending him bills marked "Please remit at once" on top, but he never received any payment.

Finally, his patience exhausted, Miller sent the free-spender a snapshot of his 4-month-old baby daughter with the message, "This is why I need the money you owe me."

Gomez sent him an enlarged snapshot of a beautiful blonde with the message: "Here's why I can't pay you!"

SLEEPING BEAUTY
A soft 10-inch prick.

* * *

Liz: Don't you ever try and kiss me that way again.
Mac: Sorry. Just a slip of the tongue.

* * *

What's the best way to make yourself last with your girlfriend?

Let everyone else go first!

* * *

Sweeney was racing down the street a mile a minute when Kevin stopped him. "What's the matter?"

"Outa my way!" he panted. "I just ran into a beautiful blonde."

"Is that any reason to race down the street like this?"

"I'll say! I ran into her husband too!"

* * *

Why does masturbating make Superman stronger?

Because he's pumping iron.

* * *

Terrence picked up Jennie in a singles bar, took her back to his place, and the two were soon in the bedroom making it hot and heavy. Afterward, lighting up a cigarette, he said, "So, how was it?"

"Boy, are you a lousy lover!" snapped Jennie.

"Oh, yeah?" said Terrence. "How can you tell that in just two minutes?"

* * *

It was a cold winter night in Minneapolis. Maurice and Grisel were out on a date when they got a flat tire. Maurice got out to change it, while Grisel stayed warm in the car. Without hat or gloves, Maurice wasn't prepared for the cold.

He quickly changed the flat and got back into the car, shivering. "You're half frozen," said the girl. "Wouldn't you like to warm your hands? Just put them between my legs."

"You know," said Maurice, "my ears are real cold too."

* * *

There once was a quarterback Viking
Whose amorous prowess was striking.
    A hell of a guy
    He could well satisfy
Any number of girls to his liking.

*   *   *

"What's the definition of a pussy?"
"A small thing covered with hair that eats tongue."

*   *   *

Geoffrey had been jilted by his girl and was being cheered up by his friend Herb.

"Don't take it too hard," consoled Herb. "I know you must be feeling pretty bad about it."

"No," said Geoffrey. "Not only did she return all my presents, but she accidentally threw in a few that some other guys gave her!"

*   *   *

Fred: Do you enjoy fornicating?
Anne: No!
Fred: Neither do I . . . let's start now so we can hurry up and get it over with!

Russ, a confirmed bachelor, was telling his closest pal, Paul, about his new conquest.

"Look," he sighed, "about a month ago I met this girl, and we've been going steady ever since. I'm crazy about her. Every time we go out, I come back liking her even more. We never quarrel, we both enjoy doing the same things, and she appreciates every little thing I do for her. You think I ought to marry her?"

"Don't be stupid!" pleaded Paul. "Why louse up a good thing?"

*   *   *

Gary and Steve, two carpenters, were on their lunch break.

"Hey," said Gary, "how'd you get that black eye?"

"Aw, I was kissing my girlfriend good night and her garter belt broke."

*   *   *

What comes out of a lecher's pecker when he kisses his girlfriend?

The wrinkles.

*   *   *

Corbett picked up Carole at a singles bar and wound up in her apartment.

"Huh!" snorted the girl. "Here you were telling me all those stories about the orgies you said you'd been to, and now that we're in bed together you can't do a thing!"

"I know, I know," muttered Corbett, "but I've never been alone with a girl before."

Howard was greeted by his date in the living room of her parents' home.

"Honey, we're gonna have a fantastic time tonight," he said. "I have four tickets to the theater."

"But why do we need four tickets?" she asked.

"Easy," he said. "They're for your mother, father, brother, and sister."

*   *   *

What's the difference between mono and herpes?

You get mono from snatching a kiss.

*   *   *

How do you screw a fat girl?

Roll her in flour and go for the wet spot.

*   *   *

SCORE PAD
A lecher's apartment.

*   *   *

Why did the guy chase his girlfriend up a tree?

So he could kiss her between the limbs!

* * *

A boy and a girl from the nudist colony were strolling in the woods when he said, "Don't look now, but I think I'm falling in love with you."

* * *

Did you hear about the businessman who gave his secretary a dress for her first week's pay?

And the next week he tried to raise her salary?

* * *

LECHER'S LAMENT

Now that I'm old and feeble, my pilot light is out.

What used to be my sex appeal is now my water spout.

I used to be embarrassed to make the thing behave,

For every single morning, it would stand and watch me shave.

But now I'm growing old, and it sure gives me the blues

To have the thing hang down my leg and watch me shine my shoes.

What's a semi-quickie?
Half-fast sex!

*   *   *

What's the difference between a fox and a pig?
At least a half-dozen beers.

*   *   *

Wink had set up the double date. He said, "You get to choose, Rocco."

"Okay," said his buddy.

"Roseanne has kind of a dumpy figure. She's short on looks, but she gives an incredible blowjob. Laurel is pretty and has a perfect pair of legs, which she shows off by wearing shoes with very high heels."

"Say no more," interrupted Rocco. "I'll go for head over heels anytime."

*   *   *

A young Pennsylvania Quaker went calling on his girlfriend, and she shyly agreed to sit on his lap. Soon he began getting an erection, so he excused himself and went out into the backyard. He took his penis out, gave it a vicious shake, and spoke to it thusly:

"Now, that is naughty! Thee must not do that! If thee does that again, I shall cut thee off!"

Down it went, and he returned to the house and picked up where he left off. Up it shot again. He excused himself once more, went out back, hauled it out, shook it fiercely and said in a stern voice, "Thee is bad! Thee must not do that! Do that again and I shall surely cut thee off!"

It diminished, and he went back in the house, where the same thing happened. Without a word, he stalked out to the backyard, pulled it out, rolled up his sleeves, spit on his hands, and said, "Lucky for thee I forgot my pocketknife. I shall jerk thee off instead!"

* * *

Marital Manics

Debbie and Ray were married in a Las Vegas chapel. An hour later they began sipping champagne in their hotel honeymoon suite.

The nervous bride said that she had a confession to make, but the groom reassured her, whispering, ''Darling, I know about the time you worked as a stripper.''

''It was before that,'' said Debbie.

''You mean even before you were on the street hustling to pay for your habit?''

''Yes, dear, and even before my sex-change operation.''

* * *

Did you hear about the bride who was so nervous she didn't know whether to say, "I do," "I have," or "I will"?

*   *   *

Is it wrong to have sex before you're married?

Only if it makes you late for the ceremony!

*   *   *

Jesse spent the morning before the wedding painting daisies all over his future bride's nude body. When he finished, he said, "Please don't wash them off until tomorrow."

"Why not?" asked the startled girl.

"Because it'll be the only way I'll be able to say I deflowered you on our wedding night."

*   *   *

How can you tell if a bride is anxious? She comes walking down the aisle!

*   *   *

A young couple from the Kentucky hills came into Louisville to get married, bringing Jethro, their best man, along. When they applied at the city hall for a marriage license, they were informed the law required blood tests before they could get a license.

"There's a doctor 'cross the street," advised the clerk. "He'll take care of you."

The M.D. took blood samples from the prospective bride and groom.

"What're yew doing this fer, Doc?" asked Jethro.

"Checking for venereal disease. If such signs are found, the wedding'll have to be postponed until it is cured."

"That a fact?" nodded the best man. "Well, ain't you gonna take a sample of mah blood?"

"What for? You're not getting married, are you?"

"No," answered Jethro. "But Ah'm gonna board with 'em!"

* * *

"You went to the wedding of those friends of yours yesterday. How was it?"

"Terrible. The groom was uncouth and loud, and the bride was so embarrassed she nearly had a miscarriage!"

Colin and Alice, a deaf and dumb couple, were married. That night in their honeymoon hotel Colin began talking to his bride in sign language. He said, "Listen, if you want to have sex just rub my pecker once. If you don't want to have sex—rub it a hundred times."

*　　*　　*

Newly-married Cora was telling a girlfriend how she had successfully taught her husband some badly needed manners. Just at that moment he dashed into the living room and said, "Come on, honey, let's fuck."

The friend sat stunned as the husband scooped his bride into his arms and carried her into the bedroom. Sometime later Cora returned, smiling and adjusting her clothing. "See what I mean?" she beamed. "A week ago he wouldn't have asked!"

*　　*　　*

Did you hear about the nudist bride who didn't go in the sun for three months—she wanted to be married in white.

*　　*　　*

Donnie and Muriel, just married, were up in their Carmel honeymoon suite on their wedding night. As they undressed for bed, Donnie tossed his pants to Muriel and said, "Here, put these on."

She put them on, but the waist was twice the size of her body and the pants fell down around her ankles. "I can't wear your pants!"

"That's right," said Donnie, "and don't forget it! I'm the man, and I wear the pants in this family."

Muriel then slipped out of her panties and threw them at her husband. "Try these on."

He tried, but they were so small he could get them on only as far as his kneecap.

"Hell, I can't get into your pants!"

"That's right," said Muriel. "And you're not going to until you change your damn attitude!"

Sounds drifting from the honeymoon suite kept the bellboy glued to the door. Between gasps a male voice moaned, ''Now will you let me?''

Throughout the night the bellboy, his ear to the keyhole, heard the same plea. As he was about to give up he heard the man croak, ''Honey, it's almost dawn. Now will you let me?''

''Oh, all right,'' sighed a sweet voice. ''Go ahead and take it out.''

* * *

MARRIAGE
A long banquet with
the dessert served first.

* * *

Charlene and Greg stopped in a small New England town to get married. They were told by the judge that it would take at least two days to obtain a license. The anxious couple looked completely dejected until Charlene offered, ''Can't you say a few words to tide us over the weekend?''

* * *

Why was Princess Di disappointed on her honeymoon?

She thought all rulers had 12 inches.

* * *

Guys at a bachelor stag party were swapping stories about their wedding nights. When his turn came, big Louie said, "On da toid day—"

"No, on the first night, what happened on the first night?" interrupted the others.

"On da toid day—" said big Louie.

"Are you drunk? We're talkin' about weddin' nights!"

"I'm tellin' ya, on da toid day she said she had to take a pee."

* * *

How can you tell Joan Collins's new husband?

He's the one with leg makeup on his ears.

* * *

What's Joan Collins's definition of a husband?

An attachment you screw on the bed.

*   *   *

VIRGIN BRIDE
A right-ring extremist.

*   *   *

Theresa and Sidney had been married for less than a year and Sidney appeared troubled.

"Darling," said the young bride, "tell me what's bothering you. We promised to share all our joys and all our sorrows, remember?"

"But this is different," protested Sidney.

"Together, darling," insisted Theresa, "we will bear the burden. Now, tell me what our problem is."

"Well," said Sidney, "we've just become the father of a bastard child."

*   *   *

What's the difference between a mistress and a wife?

The difference is night and day!

*   *   *

Why don't witches have babies?

Because their husbands have holloweenies.

A prosperous stockbroker and his wife had everything money could buy, until the market turned sour and when he lost everything. He came home that night and said to her, "You better learn to cook so we can fire the cook."

"Okay," she said, "but you better learn to screw so we can fire the chauffeur."

The delighted, incredulous bride
Exclaimed to her groom at her side
   "I never could quite
   Believe till tonight
Our anatomies *would* coincide."

NEWS ITEM

Floyd Kerdyk, of this city, was today accused of signing a false name when applying for a marriage license. The new Mrs. Kerdyk came to his defense, saying, "Floyd didn't mean to do that—it's just that he's so accustomed to registering at hotels."

The newlyweds were very grateful when his parents, Thurston and Grace, invited them to live at their house until they got on their feet. Thurston turned the attic into a real nice bedroom. On their first night at home, Thurston and Grace were in bed reading when suddenly they heard banging noises upstairs. The parents realized what was going on when the chandelier in their bedroom started shaking.

The old man said to his wife, "It's been a long time since we—" Thurston then made passionate love to Grace.

A half hour later they heard the same noises and Thurston said, "I feel ten years younger. I know I can do it again." And he took Grace for a second time.

When the chandelier began to shake and the banging was heard for a third time, the old man picked up a broomstick and began banging on the ceiling. "Hey, that's enough up there," he shouted. "You're killing your mother!!!"

Florence: What fun do you and your husband get out of getting drunk every weekend?

Josephine: Well, every time he gets lit, he thinks I'm someone else's wife and sneaks me up through the back way of our apartment!

*   *   *

Tony and Sheila went to the doctor. "I think I'm pregnant!" said Sheila.

"How many times have you missed?" asked the M.D.

Looking at her husband, Sheila replied, "I guess we haven't missed a night, have we?"

*   *   *

Dr. Margolis gave his diagnosis to the female who stood before him. "This examination reveals a serious situation. I want you to refrain from relations with your husband for several weeks. Can I count on you?"

"Sure, Doc, that's no problem. I got a boyfriend, you know."

*   *   *

Norman and Babs, who'd been married 23 years, were at a cocktail party.

"I could be all out of sorts when I get up in the morning," boasted Norman, "but as soon as I brush my teeth, I feel ten years younger."

"Why don't you try brushing them before you go to bed?" suggested Babs.

* * *

Why are so many babies so neurotic these days?

They've just come from 9 months in solitary confinement.

* * *

"Could you perhaps describe the expression on your husband's face when you're having sex?" asked the marriage counselor.

"Well, usually it's sort of contorted with tension and excitement," replied the woman, "but I remember one time when it was contorted with anger."

"With anger? When was that?"

"That was the time he was peering in through the bedroom window."

* * *

Natalie, a young advertising exec, was confiding to Lenore, an office colleague.

"My husband and I had a terrific fight last night."

"Over what?" asked Lenore.

"He was rummaging around, looking for something, and happened to find my birth-control pills," sighed the woman.

"So?"

"He had a vasectomy two years ago."

* * *

VASECTOMY
Tearing off a piece of vas.

* * *

Gaynor, the hard-driving head of a brokerage house, was advised to have a medical checkup. The doctor examined him and then asked, "How often do you have sexual intercourse?"

"Every Monday, Wednesday, and Friday," replied Gaynor.

"That's your trouble! I think that you'd be better off if you eliminated Wednesdays!"

"I can't skip Wednesdays," answered the executive. "That's the one night in the week that I'm home."

* * *

What's misery for a middle-aged woman?
Borrowing her neighbor's douche bag and finding her husband's false teeth in it!

*   *   *

The neighbor's wife told Sue Ellen, "Do you realize that yore husband is tryin' to lay me while you are pregnant?"

"So what!" snapped Sue Ellen. "Didn't Ah put out for yore Jasper when you was expecting?"

*   *   *

Did you hear about the farmer who couldn't keep his hands off his wife, so he fired them?

*   *   *

Farmer Kenyon and his wife were lying in bed one night, and he began caressing his wife's bottom. While rubbing it, he said, "If this would only lay eggs, we could get rid of the chickens."

Kenyon then started caressing her breasts, and said, "If these would only give milk, we could get rid of our cows."

She started caressing him and said, "If this would only get hard more often, we could get rid of the farmhand."

Tricia and Brett were visiting a psychiatrist and she complained that he was making her life unbearable.

"Why is your wife so unhappy?" asked the shrink.

"I don't know," replied Brett. "Every night after dinner we watch TV. Every Friday I bring her my paycheck. She has charge accounts in the department stores. Saturday night I take her out to dinner and the movies."

"Sounds reasonable," said the doctor.

"Reasonable!" fumed Tricia. "He hasn't made love to me since the day we were married!"

"Why don't you make love to your wife?" inquired the psychiatrist.

"I don't know how," said Brett.

"There are times when unusual treatment is indicated," said the shrink. He placed the young woman on the couch and began screwing her.

"Now do you understand?" inquired the M.D. when he'd finished.

"Doctor," she said, "my husband's rather thick-headed. Do you think you could show him how again?"

* * *

Allen and Gladys were having a heated argument. Finally the wife exclaimed, "I was a fool when I married you!"

"I suppose you were," replied Allen, "but I was so horny at the time that I didn't even notice."

* * *

In the traditional wedding picture, why is the groom in a chair and the bride standing?

Because he's too tired to get up, and she's too sore to sit down!

* * *

The psychiatrist asked a well-known movie star, "Do you talk to your wife during intercourse?"

He said, "Only if there's a telephone handy!"

* * *

If a woman is a nymphomaniac, what is her husband?

Tired!

* * *

What do they call a woman who doesn't practice birth control?

A mother!

*   *   *

MATE SWAPPING
Sexual four-play.

*   *   *

Hubbard married a girl whom he hardly knew. Several days after the ceremony his friend Phil found him wandering around the streets in a fit of depression.

"What happened?" asked Phil.

"Something awful," murmured Hubbard. "I'd rather not talk about it."

"Don't tell me your wife has left you already?" probed his buddy.

Hubbard shook his head.

"Then what's the matter?"

"We moved into our new apartment the other day and since then she's been going from one phone booth to another changing her number on the walls!"

*   *   *

Did you hear about the Vegas chorus girl who got her mink coat the hard way—from her husband?

What's the difference between a bad husband and a good husband?

A bad husband boxes his wife's jaw!

* * *

Age had caught up with Dooley. He was no longer the great lover he had been in his prime.

Shortly after dinner one Sunday, Dooley became distressed when his wife jealously told him that her friend could be satisfied five times nightly by her spouse.

That night the decrepit Dooley performed well the first two times, took a nap before and after the third, just barely made the fourth and fifth, then triumphantly went to sleep.

He awoke at 10 A.M. Late for work, he ran into his boss in the hall. "I don't mind your tardiness," said the boss, "but where the hell were you Monday and Tuesday?"

* * *

Irate Housewife: My husband can lick your husband.

Second Housewife: I think he does.

*   *   *

What's a good indication to a wife that her husband had a wild night?

She finds a false eyelash in his pubic hair!

*   *   *

It had been a great weekend at Wakefield's country place in Connecticut, but Erwin and Oscar had to get back to work in New York. As Erwin loaded their luggage into the car, Oscar thanked Wakefield for the pleasant stay. "You sure have a beautiful house."

"It was a pleasure having you guys here," said Wakefield.

"The last two days sure have been super," continued Oscar. "Your wife's a great cook. And she's the best in bed I've ever had."

Erwin and Oscar hopped in the car and drove off.

"What kind of a thing was that to say?" asked Erwin. "Did I actually hear you tell Wakefield that his wife was the best in bed you ever had?"

"Yeah!" said Oscar. "Truthfully, she's nowhere near the best. But Wakefield's such a nice guy, I didn't want to hurt his feelings."

Hung like a horse, Paparelli died with an erection. The funeral staff had fits trying to make him presentable. They tried strapping the appendage to his body, but it pulled him to a sitting position. They tied it to his leg, but the leg sprang up in the air.

The funeral director called Mrs. Paparelli in desperation. She told him to cut the thing off and shove it up his ass. The undertaker put down the phone and wondered why he hadn't thought of that himself.

At the funeral the widow walked by the open casket and noticed a pained expression on Paparelli's face. There was even a tear in the corner of the dead man's eye. She leaned over and whispered, "See, you bastard, I told you it hurts."

*   *   *

PENIS
A bone of contentment.

*   *   *

Alma: I think you should know—my husband will be home in about forty-five minutes.

Pete: That's all right. I haven't done anything wrong.

Alma: I know. But if you intend to, you'd better hurry.

*   *   *

Mrs. Baxter was visiting with her daughter in Palm Springs. "I can't understand it," she said. "You've been married three times and you've had dozens of boyfriends, why haven't you gotten pregnant?"

"Well, Mother," replied the girl. "To tell you the truth, I've never been able to bring myself to swallow that filthy stuff."

*   *   *

"I have to take every precaution to avoid pregnancy," confided Louise over the back fence.

"But hasn't your husband just had a vasectomy?" asked her neighbor.

"Yes—and that's why I have to take every precaution." •

*   *   *

Three daughters, Kathryn, Elizabeth, and Charlotte, were all married on the same day. Their parents listened at all the bedroom doors. They heard Kathryn laughing and Elizabeth crying, but Charlotte was completely silent. Next morning they asked why.

Kathryn: You always told me to laugh when something tickled me.

Elizabeth: You always told me to cry when something hurt me.

Charlotte: You always told me when I had my mouth full to keep it shut.

*   *   *

PETROLEUM JELLY
A sport coating.

*   *   *

When McCall's three sons were wed at the same time, he demanded that they all spend their honeymoons at his summer estate.

The morning after the triple wedding, McCall waited for his sons to show up for breakfast. Jeff, the eldest, was the first to appear.

"How often did you make love to your wife last night?"

"Three times, Dad," was the reply.

"And what did your wife say to you this morning?"

"She said, 'Good morning, darling.' "

"That's a true son of mine," he smiled. "Go right into the kitchen and have some bacon and eggs."

Just then, Nils appeared. "Well, son," called the old man, "how many times did you make love last night?"

"Four, Dad," answered the boy.

"What did she say to you this morning?"

"She said, 'Good morning, darling.' "

"Good boy! Now go join your brother for some breakfast!"

Thirty minutes later David, the youngest, came down, drawn and haggard.

"My God!" exclaimed McCall. "What happened to you?"

No answer.

"At least tell me: How many times did you make love last night?"

"Once," said the boy weakly.

"Once?" exploded the old man. "And you're supposed to be a son of mine? What did your wife say to you this morning?"

"She said, 'Get the hell off!' "

Streetwalker Snickers

To a hooker, what's the sexiest four-letter word?
Cash!

*   *   *

What do butter and a hooker have in common?
They both spread for bread.

*   *   *

A pretty young call girl stood before the judge in night court. He said, "I hereby fine you three hundred dollars for prostitution."

"Your Honor, can you give me an hour to raise the money?"

*　*　*

PIMP
For whom the belles toil.

*　*　*

A new mortuary in a tough mill town decided to advertise in an unorthodox fashion, and so draped a banner across the front of its building that read:

OUR STAFF WILL STUFF YOUR STIFF

Not to be outdone, the whorehouse across the street responded with a banner reading:

OUR STAFF WILL STIFF YOUR STAFF

*　*　*

Did you hear about the ingenious call girl who found a better-paying position?

*　*　*

How can you tell that a call girl is from a very small town?

The only thing open all night is her legs!

* * *

With the new tax laws, it seems that everybody is having problems. Bernstein, a big businessman, was being audited by the IRS. He was there all day. The investigator examined his write-offs—his entertainment expenses. When it was all over, Bernstein was so shaken he made a date with his favorite call girl.

As he finally began to unwind after a few drinks, Bernstein said to the girl, "Honey, you are in the right business. You make all that money and don't have to report it."

"Maybe so," she replied, "but I can't write anything off for depreciation."

* * *

Who's the most popular member of a horny softball team?

The designated hooker!

* * *

A notorious whore named Miss Hearst
In the weakness of men is well versed.
    Reads a sign o'er the head
    Of her well-rumpled bed:
"The customer always comes first."

*   *   *

Hiram and Abner, two Tennessee hillbillies, met behind a still.

"Howdy," said Hiram.

"Howdy," said Abner. "Ain't seen you 'round these parts in a spell. Where ya been keepin' yerself?"

"Took a vacation," said Hiram.

"Where'd ya go?" asked Abner.

"Nashville."

"Enjoy yrself?"

"Yep. Spent m'two weeks there livin' in one o' them there brothels."

"That musta been mighty costly," said Abner.

"Nope, kinfolk."

*   *   *

What do you call a guy who's just starting out as a pimp?

A rookie nookie bookie!

*   *   *

COMPLETE FAILURE

A pregnant prostitute driving an
Edsel with a Dukakis sticker on it.

* * *

The john took off all his clothes with the exception of his socks and got into bed. "You're not going to leave your socks on, are you?" said the hooker.

"You're damn right I am," he answered. "I'm not taking any chances of getting athlete's foot!"

* * *

Poor little Shanda was sobbing her heart out. "Whatsa matter?" asked her friend.

"My teacher said I'd turn out bad. My parents said I'd turn out bad. The priest said I'd turn out bad. And now the madam says I'm too nice!"

* * *

What did the hooker say to the john who claimed he had 13 inches?

"I find that hard to swallow!"

* * *

What would you call a hooker with a 500-pound john?

Pressed for cash!

* * *

On her bosom a beauteous young frail
Had illumined the price of her tail;
    And on her behind
    For the sake of the blind
The same is embroidered in Braille.

* * *

Rosalie approached her madam and informed her, "I'm quitting!"

"What's the matter?" asked the madam. "Business is good. Why, you went upstairs at least twenty times last night."

"That's the trouble," answered the girl, "my feet are just killing me!"

* * *

PROSTITUTE
A girl that don't give
a fuck for nothing

* * *

Darryl passed a house with a little red light burning in front, so he stepped inside. There was nobody in sight and nothing there but an empty hallway with two doors reading, Over 35 and Under 35.

He decided to be truthful and entered the door that said Over 35.

He found himself in another empty hall, with two more doors, reading, Over 8 inches and Under 8 inches.

Truthful again, Darryl went through the Under 8 inches door. He found another empty hall, with two more doors, reading: Once a Night and Over Four Times a Night.

Still wanting to be truthful, Darryl entered the door marked Once a Night and found himself back out in the street.

Moral: Always tell the truth, and you'll never get screwed!

Bayard, a hypersensitive Madison Avenue ad exec, was having a martini at the local watering hole. After not speaking for a while, a colleague asked, "You seem down. Anything wrong?"

"Last night I went out," he explained, "and saw this very young prostitute on the corner.

"She was lightly and poorly dressed—and it was cold. She was so young, so hungry. She must not have eaten for days. My God, her arms were so thin and cold, and her legs were thin and very cold. I really couldn't hold back my tears while I was fucking her."

* * *

What does a prostitute call her earnings? John dough!

* * *

What's the definition of a hyperactive hooker?
One who turns tricks so fast she has to hand out air-sickness bags.

* * *

A dwarf went into Sullivan's saloon, and standing on tiptoe, demanded a beer. After several brews he said to Sullivan, who was tending bar, "Hey, where can a guy get a piece of tail around here?"

"There's a whorehouse on the next block," said Sullivan, and told him how to find it.

An hour later the little fellow was back for more beer.

"Did you get fixed up okay?" asked the barkeep.

"Yep," replied the dwarf, "and did I make her yell!"

"Listen," snorted Sullivan, "don't give me that crap. How could a little runt like you make a woman yell?"

"Oh," said the dwarf, "I ran out without paying her."

*   *   *

Why was the prostitute with two boxes an outcast?

Because she walked around with a holier than thou attitude!

*   *   *

PROSTITUTE
A tollhouse cookie.

*　　*　　*

The prostie walked into the bar leading a duck on a leash. She sat down and put the duck on the bar.

"What's the idea of bringing that pig in here?" barked the bartender.

"That ain't no pig, you moron," screamed the streetwalker.

"You shut up," said the barkeep. "I'm talking to the duck."

*　　*　　*

There was a fire in a Chicago brothel, and one of the firemen came running out with a bed.

The madam screamed, "Thank God they saved the workbench!"

*　　*　　*

The mother of a 16-year-old boy said to her husband: "You've got to do something about Bill. I've found out that he's practicing self-abuse. Regularly."

Bill's father decided to take the boy downtown to Polly's Place. He rang the bell and the madam answered.

"Hi, Polly," he said. "Listen, I want you to fix my son up with a nice girl."

Then he turned to Biff. "You do whatever they say, and afterward come meet me at the bar across the street."

Half an hour later Biff arrived and his father asked, "How did it go?"

"Oh, all right, I guess," said the boy.

"You liked it, didn't you?" insisted the father.

"Yeah, a little," said Biff. "Thing is, you can't see what you're doing."

* * *

What do they call a red light district?
Erogenous Zone.

* * *

Bert worked out a financial agreement with a strange woman at a bar and then followed her up the stairs to her room. When they got inside, she took out her glass eye, removed her false teeth, wooden leg, and falsies, then proceeded to unpin the red wigs from both her upper and lower hairdos.

Bert, in a state of shock, began edging out of the room. The girl sneered, "What's the matter? Don't you like me?"

"No, no, it's nothing like that," stammered Bert, "but I think I left my tool in my other pants!"

*   *   *

What do they call coin-operated robot hookers in Las Vegas?
Slut machines.

*   *   *

BUMPER STICKER
Support free enterprise—
legalize prostitution.

*   *   *

Did you hear about the Old Testament prostitute who was arrested for trying to make a prophet?

*   *   *

The janitor in the convent was caught stealing some cash. He confessed that he had taken it from the room shared by Sister Cecelia and Sister Katherine. The Mother Superior summoned Sister Cecelia to her office and asked her what the money was doing in the room in the first place. "Oh, it's trick money," answered the nun.

"Do you show card tricks for money? If you raise funds for the convent this way, you can be easily absolved from the sin of using playing cards."

"Oh, no, Holy Mother," said Sister Cecelia. "It's Sister Katherine. She says she charges twenty dollars per trick, but I can assure you she has never even touched playing cards in her life."

* * *

Perverted Proverbs

The ice man cometh...especially if the housewife is builteth like a brick walleth.

* * *

It's easy to lie with a straight face, but it's more fun to lie with a curved body.

* * *

Put some added fun in your life.
Try a floorsome foursome.

* * *

Love is like toilet paper. After you tear off your first piece, the rest comes easy.

* * *

The difference between dark and hard is that it gets dark every night.

* * *

A bird in the hand isn't half as much fun as a hand in the bush.

* * *

Sex may be bad for one, but it's sure wonderful for two!

* * *

If it don't hang right, use a big pipe in your pants pocket as a decoy.

* * *

Unless you are pretty well balanced, don't ever try to make love in a hammock.

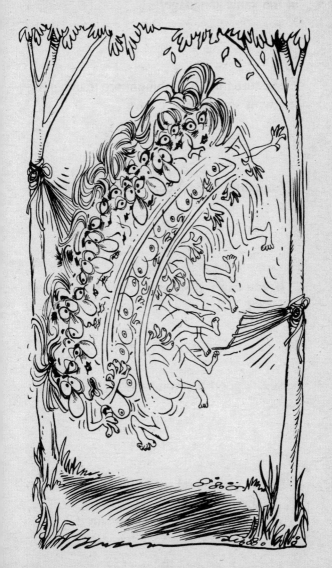

Sex is universal because everybody screws in the same language!

* * *

Masturbation is nothing more than having sex with someone you love.

* * *

Enjoy the sex act before Congress repeals it.

* * *

If you can't give up sex, get married and taper off.

* * *

Sex is good for you, and you don't need batteries.

* * *

Some girls think it's fun to fight for it . . . others just take it lying down.

* * *

When it comes to good clean fun, you can't beat a double bubble bath.

*   *   *

There's only one thing wrong with sex—it's so habit-forming.

*   *   *

The three best things in life are a martini before and a nap afterward.

*   *   *

You can't take sex with you, so wear it out before you go.

*   *   *

A well-balanced sex life is impossible in a canoe.

*   *   *

Do it now. There may be a law against it tomorrow.

*   *   *

Candy is dandy, but sex doesn't rot your teeth.

* * *

Where there's a wilt there's no way.

* * *

Gentlemen prefer blondes, because blondes know what gentlemen prefer.

* * *

The curves men view with such delight
Are often kept in drawers at night.

* * *

Some women wear black panty hose in memory of those who have passed beyond.

* * *

Sex is like the air. It's not important unless you're not getting any.

* * *

Legs are a girl's best friend, but even the best of friends must soon part.

* * *

Remember: When you say *oralgenitalism*, you've said a mouthful.

* * *

And don't ever forget:

The point of a joke is like a good piece of tail—it's no good if you don't get it.

* * *

145

College Copulators

What's the first thing a sorority girl does in the morning?
Walks home!

*   *   *

Why was the female honor student upset?
She missed a period!

*   *   *

What did the professor do for the college girl who was having trouble with Sex Ed.?
Kept her after class and pounded it into her!

* * *

A pretty young coed of Wimley
When reproached for not acting quite primly
      Answered: "Heavens above!
      I know sex isn't love!
But it's a most reasonable facsimile!"

* * *

NICE COLLEGE GIRL
One that puts it in for you.

* * *

Did you hear about the passionate UCLA coed who was barred from the beach when the lifeguard saw her going down for the third time?

* * *

"Gee," exclaimed the breathless coed to her sorority sisters about last night's panty raid. "This bruiser from the football team got me cornered, so I had to fork over my panties. What else could I do?

"Later," she went on, "I gave him the slip."

*   *   *

Sally and Nita were sitting at a campus cocktail bar having their share of liquid refreshment. Toward the end of the evening Sally remarked, "If I have another beer, I'm going to feel it."

Nita replied. "If I have another, I won't care who does."

*   *   *

A University of Iowa couple were caught in the backseat of a car. The policeman shined the light on them, turned to the boy and said, "Okay, buddy, I'm next!"

The fellow got fidgety and nervous.

"What's the matter?" asked the cop.

The boy replied, "Gee, Officer, I never did it to a cop before!"

*   *   *

Did you hear about the college kids that had a nice date?

They played Scrabble, and he licked her!

*   *   *

OVERHEARD IN LOVER'S LANE

Babs: I want you to know I've never done anything like this before.

Chip: Then you've certainly inherited a lot of talent!

* * *

There was a young coed named Fitchin
Who was scratching her crotch in the kitchen.
    Her roommate said, "Rose,
    It's the crabs, I suppose."
Rose said, "Yes, and the bastards are itchin'."

* * *

The football coach stopped a pretty coed and barked, "Young lady, what are you doing with that varsity letter on your sweater? Don't you know that it's against campus rules to wear a letter unless you've made the team?"

"Yes, sir," she said.

* * *

Peters was the midwest university's star fullback. Three days before the big game he injured his leg during a practice scrimmage. After an examination the doctors reported that he would be unable to play. The *Campus Chronicle* planned to announce the sad news with the headline: "Team Will Play Without Peters."

However, the dean found out about this attempt at college humor before the *Chronicle* went to press. He ordered the editor to change it or be kicked off the paper. The editor complied, and Friday morning the *Chronicle* hit the campus with the headline, "Team Will Play With Peters Out."

Bannick, the new coach, was being reprimanded for being verbally abusive in his handling of the football squad. He snapped at the university president, "If you don't like the way I do things, you can shit in your hat! And as for you," he snarled at the athletic director, "you can screw yourself."

After the coach left, the president said, "What are Bannick's qualifications for the job?"

"In his eight years at State before he came here," said the athletic director, "his record was seventy-seven wins, two losses, and one tie."

"Hmmm," mused the university president, "I can always buy myself a new hat—but I'd say you have a real sex problem."

*   *   *

Louise, a University of Florida soph home on a semester break, advised her younger sister, "You can never tell about school athletes. Either they're so slow you want to scream or so fast you have to."

*   *   *

Did you hear about the Penn State coed

who finally got fed up with her shy boy-friend's fumbling advances and decided to put him in her place.

* * *

ORGASM
College boy's favorite sport.

* * *

Frosh: Gosh, Ralph, everything I've been doing lately has been wrong.
Soph: Good, Jennifer! Let's you and I go out tonight!

* * *

Jay and his date were strolling through the moonlit park.

"I've heard you're very shy," he said, "but you needn't worry about making conversation. I've got a simple code that eliminates the need for talk. If you nod your head, it means you want me to hold your hand, and if you smile, it means you'd like me to kiss you. It's that easy. What do you think of my plan?"

She laughed in his face.

* * *

Why did the Michigan State senior kick his gay roommate out of the house?
He said he was a pain in the ass!

*   *   *

SIGN ON UNIVERSITY OF KANSAS
BULLETIN BOARD
For sale—good dating car. Owner needs money to buy baby buggy.

*   *   *

Colin was an old-fashioned kind of fraternity boy. He liked his women relatively inexperienced. Nadine, his blind date from the best campus sorority, lay contentedly in his arms. Colin kissed her tenderly, pushed her back gently, looked deeply into her eyes and asked, "How many were there before me?"

Nadine looked at him in silence for a long time. Minutes passed.

"Well," he said, "I'm waiting."

"Well," she replied, "I'm still counting."

*   *   *

Craig and Jim were having a few drinks at the campus grog shop.

"The girls in that Lambda Sigma sorority are a bunch of cock teasers," complained Craig.

"Right," agreed Jim. "And that's why it's known as the Halfway House."

*   *   *

Did you hear about the Vassar preppies who went on a jockey shorts raid—with the boys still in them?

And what about the professor's trifling wife who delighted in making it hard for his pupils.

*   *   *

Miss Crane, a very proper spinster instructor, was having lunch at an off-campus restaurant, sitting next to a pretty coed. The girl finished her sandwich and coffee, then settled back and lit up a cigarette. Miss Crane controlled herself for a few moments and then snapped, "I'd rather commit adultery than smoke in public."

"So would I," said the girl, "but I only have half an hour before my next class."

*   *   *

An astronomy teacher at Kings
Had his mind on heavenly things,
But his heart was on fire
For a coed in the choir
Who moved like jelly on springs.

*   *   *

Jane, a plain-looking coed home on summer vacation, calmly confessed to her mother than she had lost her virginity last semester.

"How did this happen?" gasped the parent.

"Well, it wasn't easy," she admitted, "but three of my sorority sisters helped hold him down."

*   *   *

Steffi's mother was worried about the way Steffi had been acting. She watched as her 19-year-old sexpot sophomore stretched out on the sofa reading a sexy book. Suddenly the girl's pelvis started to undulate and spasms overtook her as she grabbed for her crotch with one hand and her left breast with the other. Steffi shuddered, cried out, and fainted.

Steffi was taken to the family doctor and her mother explained to him what had happened. After a lengthy examination the physician said, "I think she has mechanical trouble, Mrs. Dawson."

"*Mechanical* trouble?"

"Yes," whispered the M.D. "Your daughter is coming unscrewed."

* * *

Frenzied Frolicking

Why is Valentine's Day the horniest holiday?
Because everybody has a heart on!

*　　*　　*

Why do people like Dial?
It's happiness spelled backward.

*　　*　　*

What two things in the air can make a woman pregnant?
Her legs.

*   *   *

Did you hear about the shepherd who was growing bored in the fields and decided to bury himself in his work?

*   *   *

NYMPHO
A gal who'd rather be
under a man than a hair dryer.

*   *   *

Why is a pretty girl like a ripe peach?
A man can hardly wait to get to the pit.

*   *   *

What goes in hard and pink and comes out soft and sticky?
Bubble gum!

*   *   *

What's the difference between an old cat and a kitten?
An old cat can scratch and claw, but a little pussy never hurt anyone!

*   *   *

What's the worst thing about having AIDS?
You have to leave your friends behind.

*   *   *

While performing a vasectomy on Granger, Dr. Delacorte's hand slipped and he cut off one of the man's testicles. To avoid a malpractice suit, Delacorte decided to replace the missing ball with an onion.

Several weeks later the patient returned for a checkup.

"How's your sex life?" asked the M.D.

"Okay," said Granger. "But I've had some weird side effects."

"Like what?" queried the doc.

"Every time I piss, my eyes water. When my girl gives me a blowjob she gets heartburn. And every time I pass a hamburger stand, I get a hard-on."

*   *   *

Why does everybody masturbate?
Because we all know that if you want something done right, you have to do it yourself!

*   *   *

What's the best way to stop the stork?
Shoot it in the air!

*　　*　　*

What did the reporter say after he interviewed 200 virgins?
"Today, life was just a poll of cherries!"

*　　*　　*

Did you hear about the Florida virgin who finally decided she wanted to get some experience under her belt?

*　　*　　*

What did one boob say to the other boob?
"We better stop hanging so low, they'll think we're nuts!"

*　　*　　*

KISS
An application for a better position.

*　　*　　*

What's a birth control pill?
The other thing a girl can put in her mouth to keep from getting pregnant!

＊　＊　＊

Lem and Clyde, two Georgia farmers, met on a dusty back road one morning.

"Howdy," said Lem.

"Mo'nin'," said Clyde.

"Git yer spring plantin' done yet?"

"Nope."

"How come?" asked Lem.

"Tractor's broke."

"Who broke it?"

"Hired hand," said Clyde.

"Same one that knocked up yer daughter Ella Mae?"

"Yep."

"Clumsy varmint, ain't he?"

＊　＊　＊

One ovary said to the other ovary, "Hey, did you order any furniture?"

"No, why?"

"Because there's a couple of nuts outside trying to shove an organ in."

＊　＊　＊

What did the fat nun say when her bra strap broke?

"My cup runneth over!"

* * *

What did the priest say after the nun gave him a big, wet, French kiss?

"This is one habit I'd definitely like to get into!"

* * *

Did you hear about the new pill called Valspan, half Valium and half Spanish fly?

Makes you want it bad as hell, but if you don't get any, you don't give a damn!

* * *

What's Spanish Human?

A new insecticide that makes flies so horny they screw themselves to death.

* * *

There once was a fellow called Babbitt
Who made love to a girl as a habit;
    But he ran for the door
    When the girl asked for more
And explained, "I'm a man, not a rabbit."

* * *

Dennis and Joyce were out on a date one night. Dennis drove so slowly Joyce began getting fidgety. She decided to motivate him. "Listen," she offered. "Every time you speed up the car ten miles an hour, I'll take off a piece of clothing."

Dennis pressed down the accelerator and off came the shoes. Then Joyce's skirt, blouse, bra, and finally her panties. Dennis got so excited he lost control of the car. It crashed through a fence and rolled over three times. Joyce was thrown clear but Dennis was pinned in the car.

Joyce, completely naked, had to go for help! She grabbed his shoe and held it to her crotch, then ran to a service station and began to explain, "My boyfriend is stuck—"

The mechanic said, "Lady, if he's up that far, I'll never get him out."

How can you tell if Dolly Parton forgot to wear her bra?

There are no wrinkles in her face!

* * *

What did Cinderella sing to her impotent lover?

"Someday my prince will come!"

* * *

Did you hear about the girl who took her vibrator to the beach so she could shake and bake?

* * *

Sister Margaret, a novice nun, complained to the Mother Superior about the foul language being used by the construction workers building an addition to the convent.

"Don't be upset, my child," said the older nun. "Those men may be rough, but they're good and honest and God-fearing. They simply call a spade a spade."

"No they don't," replied the young nun. "They call it a friggin' shovel!"

* * *

How do you know when you're really stoned on booze?

Somebody tells you to go screw yourself and it sounds like a good idea!

* * *

SOUND OF AN ORGY
The din of iniquity.

* * *

Chuck was in bed with an extremely fat girl. He made a jab at it.

"Wrong wrinkle!" she called.

Chuck made another try. Again, "Wrong wrinkle!"

He tried again, and another, "Wrong wrinkle!"

"Well, dammit, piss," he cried, "and I'll follow it upstream like a trout!"

* * *

What did the nymphomaniac do when the basketball team bus broke down in front of her house?

She put 'em all up!

* * *

What's pink and moist and split in the middle?

A grapefruit!

*   *   *

How do you find out who gives the best blowjobs?

Word of mouth!

*   *   *

Andersen was told by his boss, Fiske, to cut his two-person division in half. That meant he had to fire either Jack or Jill, both of whom he deeply respected.

Andersen called Jill into his office. A few seconds later the beautiful young woman stormed out of Andersen's office, grabbed her purse, and left the building.

Fiske cornered Andersen and said, ''I see you decided to fire Jill!''

''No, sir, I never got that far.''

''What do you mean?'' asked his boss.

''Well, all I said was, 'Jill, I don't know whether to lay you or Jack off,' and she was gone!''

*   *   *

What's a premature ejaculation?
A spoilt spurt!

* * *

When do you know premature ejaculation is a problem?
When you start squirting while she's still flirting!

* * *

ANALINGUS
Tongue-in-cheek.

* * *

How does an airline stewardess ask for cunnilingus?
"Put *this* over your nose and mouth and breathe normally."

* * *

Did you know that in China there are more children born every minute than in India, and in India there are more children born than in Turkey?
Which proves, more people talk turkey in India than in Turkey.

Randy hated to fly, so he took the train from Chicago to Los Angeles. After settling into his upper berth, he realized that his toupee was missing. Randy was groping around in the berth below when a woman uttered a scream.

"What are you doing?" she demanded.

"I'm sorry," apologized Randy, "but I lost my toupee."

"Well, that isn't it," she snapped.

"I know that," he said. "Mine was a new one. It didn't have a hole in it!"

What's the difference between a stickup and a holdup?

About 25 years.

*　　*　　*

If our ancestors came over on a boat, how did syphilis come over?

On the captain's dingy.

*　　*　　*

Who's the most popular guy at the nudist masquerade party?

The one who comes dressed as a gasoline pump!

*　　*　　*

What's a nymphomaniac?

A fuckaholic!

*　　*　　*

What's the difference between a woman and a volcano?

A volcano never fakes eruptions!

*　　*　　*

Why did the girl go to the nude beach?

To snatch a few rays!

Dirty Danny sat in the back of his first-grade class. Miss Pagnozzi announced, "We're going to play a game. I'll say a few words about something and you try to tell me what I'm thinking about. The first thing is a fruit. It's round and it's red."

Little Billy raised his hand and said, "An apple."

"No, it's a tomato. But I'm glad to see you're thinking," said the teacher. "Now, the next one is yellow and it's a fruit."

Rickey raised his hand and said, "A grapefruit!"

"No, it's a lemon. But I'm glad to see you're thinking," said Miss Pagnozzi. "The next one is round and it's a green vegetable."

Little Mary shouted up, "It's a lettuce."

"No," said the teacher. "It's a pea. But I'm glad to see you're thinking."

Just then Danny raised his hand and said, "Teach, can I ask you one?"

"All right."

"I got somethin' in my pocket. It's long and it's hard and it's got a pink tip."

"Danny!" shouted the teacher. "That's disgusting!"

"It's a pencil," said Danny. "But I'm glad to see you're thinking."

* * *

How is a pecker like a woman's panties?
A couple of good yanks will get them off!

* * *

Did you hear about the new deodorant called Umpire?
It's for foul balls.

* * *

PRUDE
A female who doesn't drink,
doesn't smoke and
only curses when it slips out.

* * *

What would you call an airline pilot with girlfriends in New York City and Washington, D.C.?
A shuttlecock!

* * *

What's the difference between frustration and panic?
Frustration is the first time you discover

you can't do it the second time.

Panic is the second time you discover you can't do it the first time.

* * *

What's the most fun at a picnic?

Getting the nod to put your prod in the pod of a nice broad on the warm sod!

* * *

Who was the first frankfurter entrepreneur?

Eve! She made Adam's hot dog stand!

* * *

What do you call making love hot-dog style?

A weenie between the buns!

* * *

Why did the nymphomaniac only make love doggie style?

It was the only position her doggie knew!

* * *

The small midwest town offered very little social life, so when Bernadine, the new schoolteacher, was invited for dinner at the apartment of Lillian, another teacher, she quickly accepted. After the meal Bernadine got up the courage to ask, "What do you do for sex around here?"

"I'll show you," replied the older teacher.

She whistled and a German shepherd bounded into the room. Lillian lifted her skirt and the dog started lapping her furiously between the legs. Soon the dog began to get an erection and tried to mount. The teacher slapped him hard across the face and ordered him out of the room.

"I don't understand," said Bernadine. "That thing of his looked so inviting. Why don't you let him do it to you?"

"Are you kidding? With all those kids to cope with every day, the last thing I want to do when I come home is deal with puppies!"

*   *   *

How big an ego does Burt Reynolds have?

In bed he screams his own name when he comes.

*   *   *

MINE SHAFT
What Arnold Schwarzenegger calls
his penis.

*   *   *

Why did Liz Taylor's friends buy her a
dictionary?
She didn't understand there was a difference between being "coupled" and being
"engaged."

*   *   *

Why did Dolly Parton's kids have plastic
surgery?
To get rid of the stretch marks around
their mouths.

*   *   *

CALIFORNIA BUMPER STICKER
Help bring some love into the world:
Fuck someone today!

*   *   *

How do you get a date with a mermaid?
Drop her a line!

*   *   *

Wally finally got work driving a bus through the back roads of Mississippi.

It was his first day on the job, when out in the middle of nowhere a tire blew. In addition, two wheels were in the ditch and he couldn't get the wheel cover off. As Wally worked barehanded on the clamped cover, a pretty young gal came out of her farmhouse. She watched him working without tools and said, "Wanna screwdriver?"

"Might as well," said Wally. "I ain't gonna get this damn wheel cover off."

What did the masochist say to her date?
"Slap, or I'll stop you!"

* * *

Why is a penis like a payday?
It can't come too often!

* * *

Why is credit like sex?
Because the people who need it the worst can't get it!

* * *

SINGLES BAR
A meet market.

* * *

Why is sex like a bank account?
Because you lose interest after withdrawal!

* * *

What's the problem with oral sex?
The view.

* * *

How can you tell if a girl bathes in vinegar?

She's the one with the sour puss!

*   *   *

What would you get if you crossed Continental and Air Lingus?

Connilingus.

*   *   *

What would you get if General Mills merged with Alitalia?

Genitalia.

*   *   *

What are three two-letter words that mean small?

Is it in?

*   *   *

Dwight, Louie, and Jeff lounged on the Malibu beach, rating girls. An average-looking brunette walked by.

"She's a five," said Dwight.

"A six," countered Louie.

"No, she's a one," said Jeff.

Soon a pretty redhead sashayed by.

"She's an eight," said Dwight.

"A seven," voted Louie.

"No, she's a three," said Jeff.

Finally, a gorgeous blonde strutted past.

"That's a ten, for sure!" exclaimed Dwight.

"An eleven, at least," insisted Louie.

"No, she's a six," proclaimed Jeff.

"How did you come up with six?" asked Louie.

"Well, I use the Budweiser scale," replied Jeff. "That's how many Clydesdales it would take to drag her off my face."

* * *

About the Author

This is the 42nd "Official" joke book by Larry Wilde. With sales of more than 10 million copies, it is the biggest-selling humor series in publishing history.

Larry Wilde has been making people laugh for over 30 years. As a stand-up comedian, he has performed in top night spots with stars such as Debbie Reynolds, Pat Boone, and Ann-Margret.

His numerous television appearances include *The Tonight Show, The Today Show, Merv Griffin,* and *The Mary Tyler Moore Show.*

Larry's two books on comedy technique, *The Great Comedians Talk About Comedy* (Citadel) and *How the Great Comedy Writers Create Laughter* (Nelson-Hall), are acknowledged as the definitive works on the subject and are used as college textbooks.

A recognized authority on comedy, Larry is also in constant, nationwide demand on the lecture circuit. He speaks to corporations, associations, and medical facilities on the positive effects of laughter in his keynote, "When You're Up to Your Eyeballs in Alligators."

Larry Wilde is the founder of National Humor Month, celebrated across the U.S. to point up the valuable contribution laughter makes to the quality of our lives. It begins each year on April Fools' Day.

He lives on the northern California coast with his wife Maryruth.